The Wise and Foolish Builders

The Wise and Foolish Builders

poems

Alexandra Teague

A Karen & Michael Braziller Book
PERSEA BOOKS / NEW YORK

Persea Books, Inc.
277 Broadway
New York, NY 10007

Library of Congress Cataloging-in-Publication Data
Teague, Alexandra, 1974–
[Poems. Selections]
The wise and foolish builders : poems / Alexandra Teague.
        pages ; cm
"A Karen & Michael Braziller Book."
Includes bibliographical references and index.
ISBN 978-0-89255-460-7 (original trade pbk. : alk. paper)
I. Title.
PS3620.E42A6 2015
811'.6—dc23
                        2015002090

First edition
Printed in the United States of America
Designed by Rita Lascaro

Contents

Stanzas of 13 lines — Modified Crown of Sonnets

"A colossal structure embodying the architecture of many Nations and presenting a rare study in the building art stands a great questionmark in a sea of apricot and olive orchards five miles west of San Jose . . . It is known as the 'Winchester Place,' and is the theme of many weird stories without foundation . . ."

SAN JOSE MERCURY AND HERALD, 1911

"According to some sources, the Boston Medium consulted by Mrs. Winchester explained that her family and her fortune were being haunted by spirits . . . [of those] killed by Winchester rifles. Supposedly the untimely deaths of her daughter and husband were caused by these spirits . . .

. . . Mrs. Winchester was instructed to move west and appease the spirits by building a great house for them."

THE WINCHESTER MYSTERY HOUSE WEBSITE

"each of us builds, rock by rock,
being or not being according to luck,
fate, darkness, the steps of the ghost"

EUGENIO MONTEJO, "HAMLET'S HOUR,"
KIRK NESSET, TRANSLATOR

The Wise and Foolish Builders

Claims

*I didn't see anything. I didn't hear or smell or feel anything. But when
I entered Sarah's bedroom, I understood. I understood why Sarah
had to keep building. I also think that I understand her as a person.*
THE SPIRIT SIGHTINGS LOG, WINCHESTER MYSTERY HOUSE

Now we all want your hand's ice
on the backs of our necks; your voice
whispering *No exit, No exit . . . You are
safe. . . . Go, go, go awaaay.* We came
for this—ghosts disappearing into walls
like pocket doors sliding on invisible rails;
blur of figures blooming behind the daisy
pane; cold rush of wind in the hallway.
We want you to play our pulse like piano
keys in long-locked rooms—rising arpeggio,
then falling. We feel chosen. We feel
alive: waiting like the servants for your call,
taking pictures of ourselves to glimpse your face.

peater   *- Villanelle   Perf. use of form*

Where is the military genius to grasp this terrible engine?
Oliver Winchester writes. This gun that can be loaded
on Sunday and fired all week. This gun that makes a man

the equal of a company each minute, a regiment in ten,
a full brigade in thirty. This daylight full of lead—
where is the genius to grasp it? *This terrible engine*

that can sink in a river, fire like it's never been
wet? *A resolute man on horseback* can travel west
for a month of Sundays: this gun makes a man

always ready. So He Cannot Be Captured. No weapon
more effective in the world, its aim more deft.
Where is the military genius to grasp this terrible engine—

to look past its sometimes misfires, its uneven
first trials? To see *like history it repeats itself* (and yes,
sometimes stutters). To fire *The Gun* makes a man

almost certain of safety. Against grizzly or Injun,
unequaled. Packed safe as a church nave. And yet
where is the military genius to grasp this terrible engine?
Load it on Sunday; fire all week. This gun makes a man.

Artizan Street, New Haven, 1850s: Sarah Winchester Reflects

There was always something being built
in my father's shop and sawdust tracked
onto our floors: a shimmer like the boards
becoming mist, like on the Quinnipiac
where my parents met. You could walk into
rivers then and come out with new beliefs.

> In the clock shops, time divided, shifting
> us forward notch by tiny notch. People
> crowded the Public Bathhouse—vapors
> and lye and seawater. Small salvations.
> From my French tutor: *pere* and *bois*.
> What paid for my lessons: fine houses
> ornamented by my father's careful hands.

Carriage works, mills, the boarding houses
spilling into the streets. We lived comfortably
then. My sister, the only one buried. I carried
her name, like the railway bringing New Haven
outside its skins: the custom house, the Green,
elms and soot. Factories for shirts and guns.

Room after room, new girls from Ireland
cut stacks of piecework—collar and breast,
right, back—then stitch by stitch, created
a more perfect wholeness. The country
was coming apart. Rumors. Repeating
guns. But also beauty. New planed maple.

> Everyone wanted spindles and tracery,
> moldings copied from Queen Victoria
> and The Crystal Palace. History turned against
> its lathe, shaving us loose. On my father's
> floor: pedals for organs waiting for the music
> to be built around them. No one told me
> to want a more solid world.

The House That Doesn't Grow

Mrs. Winchester was told . . . the reason a person dies
is because that person does not continue to build additions to the house
in which she lives. The spirit rots in the house that doesn't grow.
    HARRY HOUDINI

The spirit rots in the house that doesn't grow, A₁
and so the builders build a hall of mirrors—dazzling as ice refracted back to snow—
then wall it in (reflections scare the ghosts) A₂

and start a staircase in the dining room below
each step an inch toward heaven, nothing more . . . that infinite ascent, measured and slow . . .
The spirit rots in the house that doesn't grow,

and so the roofers roof the chimney hole,
then frame a ballroom with a stained-glass door (imported on a ship to riverboat)
then brick it in (blue light unnerves the ghosts)

and hang two windows etched with Shakespeare quotes:
These same thoughts people this little world.   *Wide unclasp the table of their thoughts.*
The spirit rots in the house that doesn't grow,

and so the workers work all night to close
the seventh cupola before the coming storm, their windchime hammers ringing in the cold,
then open it (the dark disturbs the ghosts)

then close it back, unnail the hallway cove;
then, for the flowers watered through the floor: a long zinc trough to catch the overflow.
The spirit rots in the house that doesn't grow
restless as a child (whose crying wakes the ghosts)

the addition-building

Claims

We take pictures of ourselves to glimpse your face,
veiled now by nonexistence: a white light in the lace
leaves of the roses. Shimmer in the curtains, glow
in the corner of the drying shed where you stowed
plums from the summer air; where once you hid
from a photographer until you almost dehydrated.
I imagine the irony would not escape you. Your voice
tells a woman she'll recover from a fever, and she does.
You blow cold breezes in the Hall of Fires—your hearths
no longer blazing; your arthritis healed. Being boneless,
you float through rooms or lie in bed—the sheets
hover over nothing. You follow tour groups to see
the last one out fall suddenly. Her camera: *a million pieces.*

The last one out falls suddenly, her camera: *a million pieces*;
the last one by the thirteenth clothes hook at the thirteenth hour freezes
as silk brushes her skin. The last one lingers for organ music
in the Venetian ballroom—*Italian, of course*—the faint click
of heels whirling. The last caretaker turns off every light,
locks the doors, and sees, above—incandescent and impossible—
the third floor blazing. The last one dreams each night it's night:
she's in the house. A voice hums *You will be believe. Believe. Believe.*
The last one down the stairs feels her hair pulled—*my mysteriously
hair moved.* The last one—after the gates are closed—arrives
to see a figure walking down the palm-lined gravel drive.
She had on a big white old-fashioned dress with a veil and a high neck.
The last one turns: *Everywhere I looked, I saw reflections of unreal objects.*

Rehearsed by Sorrows

New Haven, Connecticut, 1881

Already, you woke with sand
in your eyes each morning. Blank white
desert of the sheets. A thousand paces
from the dresser to the bed, a chasm.
The Persian rug's plateau stretched on
for days. Unsweepable light
the maid kept breaking on the floor.
On the stairs: spillways of stained glass,
slow green rapids. In your ribs, a globe's rusted axis,
a continent turned to the same intractable sun.
Dust reticulating everything. Grey evergreens
against glass. All that space
for silence inside the piano's sounding board.

How It Happened

He left to die
in a good sanitarium,
not like the one in my hometown
in an old hotel where Dr. Baker played
calliope on the roof—the air pressed up
into sound like the body pressed toward heaven
or wherever bodies go—and it didn't matter: the good
sanitarium or the nurses with their deft and patient hands
and the sheets bleached of blood and folded back: he went to
die as people do, with their inglorious glass bottles of morphine
or glasses of water Dr. Baker called a cure, so people paid to
come and sip it on the balconies. The weaker their hands,
the harder they held it—like something precious, good
enough to live for. Near the end, everything's heaven:
the fireflies on the sunken hills, the winding up
of clocks, the music from the roof, played
with a mad joy like God's hometown
is winning briefly, or a sanitarium
is just a circus where we die.

Range

Is this then how I, atheist, pacifist, drove
to the indoor gun range, swung open
into fear, gas-heater tinged; rifles and scopes
and bullet boxes—men I'd never hoped

would show me how to hold my body
forward, bend my knees, my fingers free
of the trigger because we never know, we
never know our own hands truly.

Each new part fallible, nameable—grip
and safety catch, firing pin. My friends
asking to hold 38s, sighting steady as if this
world without a god were also without spirit,

as if we were safe as houses. The bullet
casings glittering in unswept lanes, the targets
pulleyed out: bullseyes and torsos, the heart
we were supposed to, but how could I?, aim at,

though my friends pulled the trigger: ragged holes
dark in the outer circles, my ears muffled, full
of the noise, then nothing. *Is* it love that calls
us to the things of this world—the angels

of laundry rising with earthly wind, swaying
riddled on wires, or *love the hunter has for living
things, which he can only express by aiming
his gun at them?* And how do we stand wanting

to see inside this skin, not knowing what
we hope to see—where the soul is, if it
is? The clack of keys that stick, the shots
marking paper we can't repair, an eBay post

a man in England had to pull because *souls,*
spirits, and ghosts are not allowed for sale
though churches wrote to trade him the well-
spring of salvation, and as a struggling musician he'd will

the buyer royalties from any songs he'd write.
I'm very creative, he said, *but creativity's not sometimes*
without its drawbacks. We're called, too, to what defies
us to love it. The body's target hanging high

in the dim lane and the gun in my hands heavier
than it looked even unloaded, reloaded, the paper
swaying in the still air before me, not the end or
beginning, but now: both this bang and this whimper.

Stereoscope: Annie Oakley and Sarah Winchester

It began with necessity:
hunting rabbits behind a mortgaged house
then word spread out:
snow on the fields glinting off
sky, and everything narrowed:
hard wood and steel—
me, the small miracle
at the trigger men bet against:

cards riddled like windows
on a train that will take you
over oceans if you want it to;
the prince of Senegal sending
offers of tigers, and the German
kaiser sitting rigid as a portrait: ash
of his cigarette streaking the bullet
as it crumbled that one speck

of fire. Such trust in common
stranger's (woman's) hands;
The legends made them safe
the way they do: the little sure
shot, dressed to kill, meaning
dressed to shoot at nothing
alive now. I became
something to be braved, boasted

as any woman should—
holding her gun naturally as a baby
slung from her body. Love
has nothing to do with that
or it does, but also
wanting to trust something—
also our bodies bare as skinned
rabbits, and the floor cold

How can I explain
its windows designed from guns:
levers and latches aimed at
the garden's gazing ball
not for safety but because
that's how I knew to build. Not a spider,
silking out her body's web,
but a woman standing there

where the wind's eye watches
without sleeping—safe as houses
they say, but what is safe about
this world with holes shot through and
with empty safes and chairs—this
dust and light on the piano, the smoke
and no one else to warm at the hearth
now: only my own body

glass between me and the day:
not ghosts, but not the living either.
The legends grew like hedges
tangled and vined around me; words,
the spirits I started to believe in
because what else is a house but
something that holds time,
something to forgive us,

sleepless walks through rooms
held in some other world
we've built board by board; the window
open or closed and us still standing
waiting
wanting someone to see us
wanting—something soft as
silk, so maybe we are spiders

where the bed isn't, and all
the pretty ways later we sell
to the world what began
with necessity

after all—this web around us,
plums in the orchards, morning
filling up the glass: something beautiful
in every corner. How can I explain it?

The House That Doesn't Grow

The spirit rots in the house that doesn't grow,
the rigid pole lamps yellowing the light
inside familiar rooms where shadows fold

the corners back around us. Bodies close,
teacups and reading braced against the night,
the spirits in the house that doesn't grow.

What difference could it make as we grow old
to have a child, dollhouse, strings of Christmas lights
inside familiar rooms where shadows fold?

Could we outgrow ourselves? Have we outgrown
the passed-down furniture, the wakened nights
that the spirit rots in the house that doesn't grow?

Or is this house a story we've been told?
Persephone sequestered from the living light
inside familiar rooms where shadows fold.

And still we welcome shelter from the cold,
the narrow loveseat and the reassuring light,
nights in familiar rooms where shadows fold
dark leaves around the house that doesn't grow.

Sarah Winchester, 46 Years Dead, Talks to Andy Warhol

If it had been only fifteen minutes,
like a train paused at a station,
the conductor collecting the tickets
of strangers to enter
my life. If I could have been a wall:
a hundred changed faces, *simple*
and quick and chancy, as you say.
Like a blue moon, a weathervane
on the highest tower. If the wind
had turned. If anyone had
asked. Even then, in the first years
of movies, it wasn't their flicker
but *the way things happen in life*
that's unreal. Those faces glowing
in our minds. The door opening,
then death. Even before television,
it was all television: *Recluse defies*
the wrath of spirits. Mrs. Winchester fears
a second flood like Noah's wife. If it
had been a real ark and not
a houseboat. If I had duplicated
my husband, my daughter,
myself. If we could choose
what gets magnified—not the door
opening, the shot, the chafe
we cannot shake of touch. If we
were silk and paint—a house
before the earthquake. Not flashes
in a hall of mirrors. Not rumors
we start to believe of ourselves.

Claims

Everywhere I looked, I saw reflections of unreal objects:
The Thai International Hospital where my love's luck
hung from an IV pole, a bubble of air in his blood. *It could kill
him, right?* The nurses smiled and brought numbered pills.
Pills with letters. *Sawadee kha, good morning. Hello, sawadee kha.*
I knew they didn't understand. They changed the gauze
and smiled, smiled and changed the sheets. For days,
I dialed recorded voices: *The wait time is approximately. The wait
time is.* And so, at first it was a comfort when I dreamed
that night I met you in your vast, impossible, and real
house. The gaslights lit to welcome guests, you wore cotillion
lace. You took my hand and led me up the stairs that wound
and wound. Then turned: your face bloodless, ancient, dead.

They return: their faces bloodless, ancient, dead:
an *appropriate time-frame butler*. A maid carrying folded
laundry down the folded hall. A carpenter on a ladder
who doesn't know you've died, he's died—the clatter
of hammers hammering on. *When I realized he was dead,
I turned to talk to him again but he was gone.* A woman in bed.
A woman in the window. A horse grazing by the fence—
*visibly agitated but not making any noise. Like a horse in a silent
movie.* A face in the Tiffany glass. *All of a sudden—BOOM—
ghost out of nowhere. Red eyes.* Another tour passing the room,
loud-voiced, invisible. *A goast on the back porch.* A bloody knife.
*I am not a religious person who believes in God or the afterlife,
but I know what I saw and I will never again come back.*

Fortune

I didn't want to know, and still I went.
Or desperate to know, I went. Or
I was cold, and her light was warm and blinked,

a palm with fingers spread, neon and pink
against the Kansas City dark. Like something
trying to touch me, bless me, stop me

each night walking home by snow in empty
swimming pools, a rusted wheel big enough
to stand in. My mother dying, better, feverish,

drifting into the end before the end. I wished
her healed. I wished her gone, the way the city
had wished the starlings gone: cannons

blasting their roosts all fall with sound.
On repeat: distress calls. A hawk-shaped kite
flown up into the trees. The twilight, ringing,

anxious. Inside, Christmas lights stringing
February walls. Madame Someone tilting
my palm beneath a fringed silk lamp.

Thin creases for life, head, heart—the slant
toward loss or luck, an Etch-a-Sketch ready
for erasure. Did I want her to see my lies?

Dark mornings when I'd danced all night?
White cells multiplying? What could she say
but what she said? *You must expect great changes.*

The Door to Nowhere

opens to somewhere
twenty feet above the garden
air thick with star
jasmine and peonies (headache
cures) fan palms' castanet
clatter and the crescent
hedge, an ornamental
scythe, curving toward
death,
and you like Damocles inverted
from a web's
thread above its point,
each morning the same
legends and hammers
building
other stairs down
inside the hall and out
the balcony roses
(for the eyes) and the real moon,
distant and full,
outlasted dark like a door
knob's cold porcelain
you can't
turn to wherever whoever
waits on the other side

Claims

We know what we saw, and we'll never come back,
although we do—our visitations charted on a graph
of spiked blue lines. We crowd the gun museum and vote
for who should play you in the movie—Jennifer Love Hewitt,
Angela Lansbury, Holly Hunter, Meryl Streep, or Britney Spears.
We love the ways you won't be understood. Our deepest fears
made safer by the labyrinth of your life. We're not as lost,
as haunted, lonely as the light you shone to mark the coast
of you. A different bedroom every night. Two months
and maps to move your furniture. Now we're the moths
with flashlights in the midnight rooms. The city over-sprawls
your psychic sprawl, and still, *Woman much missed, you call
to us, call*—saying we are not ever only as we are.

You call to us—saying you were not ever only who you are:
the hunched old woman in the gift shop chair; the limbo bar
across the séance door to block the ghosts; a widow walking
the infinite walk of grief. You've kept three centuries talking,
our unceasing words building new stories inside old. Gold keys
in buckets, the midnight balls, the president you refused to see.
We dream you now instead of knocking. You come vampiric
from the tropic air beside my bed but do not bite. I know my luck:
the man I love survived. And still I claim you, having lived for years
between the vast unfinished walls death tears down, builds, tears
down, and builds inside our hearts. I've waited, too, for voices
calling on disconnected lines. You offer hope: the Hobson's choice
to lead our haunted lives. The warmth that lingers after your hand's ice.

Clue

Always Miss Scarlet: made to burn—satin
train of her dress, and the slender cigarette,
a magic wand in its pearl holder. Her name

like talons. Impervious, sleek as chaises longues
at the Excelsior Hotel where Diamond Bessie
glittered toward death. Always the black waterfall

of her hair (a single picture in a secret envelope).
Always the first to go, but not for this. Wicked
swish of her skirt, long red nails like the women

typing features at my father's office: brazen clack
and bells to signal each return. New questions
to narrow truth until it fit on three cards. Always,

the diagonal glide through walls, knowing before
I understood the double wick of her candlestick:
polish and gleam, victim and victimizer, knife

and ballroom. Unafraid. Every death resolvable.
Gloved and gorgeous in the pageless library,
the parlor, the conservatory: a memory palace

where she could only remember by entering
the past with her body, gathering the rope
and wrench, gathering guilt before innocence.

The Journalists Set the Record Straight on Sarah Winchester

The medium was a woman was a man who told Sarah after
she'd lost one daughter two daughters to a rare disease   a
common disease   and then her husband   son of Oliver
of William   the inventor of the rifle   founder of the company
to move West to a house with nine rooms   six rooms   sixteen
rooms   and hire carpenters to keep building   to appease the
ghosts confuse the ghosts   provide an all-consuming hobby
for her health   for William's health they tried to save   halfway
to California when he turned back   he never left home   died
at the house they were building   had built   died in a
sanitarium   and her so grief-stricken she went to Boston
to a medium   a Spiritualist   named Adam Coons   a woman
who said *Move West* so in   1882   84   85   86   she came
alone   with her sisters   knew nothing of architecture
was one of America's first women architects   an original
artist   her workmen terrified of her   grateful   she treated
them like family   turned away even Teddy Roosevelt   the
dentist   she wanted to bite him   generous to charity   *all
that a good woman should be   and nothing she should not
be*   her safe full of gold plates   almost empty except
her husband's woolen underwear   her daughter's hair   she
built every second til her own death   in 1922   til the 1906
earthquake   predicted   unexpected   convinced she had
angered the spirits   she left all the damage   the way they
had ordered   in homage to her workers   in madness   in
fear after being trapped in a room   she moved to a houseboat
an ark   believed in a flood   six months   years on the water
never left San Jose   needed hammers to live   died despite
them   drew blueprints for rooms   on the backs of old letters
butcher paper   newspaper   of this no record remains.

American Progress

after the painting by John Gast, 1872

She's billow and ravel—cumulous spume of angel
dressed for seduction: *yes, you, settler:*
follow. Bared legs eclipsing fields as she strides: glides
snow-blind white over dun plains—the stagecoach,
oxen, smoke-streaked train all racing West off
the canvas. She's bringing light—stringing the thin wire
to bind you. *Telegraph me. Telephone me. Call anytime.*
The pine trees winnowing to poles beneath her;
horses whinnying as pitch-faced, shirtless chiefs
look up and flee her. She'll show them *brave.*
She'll show them brazen: electric lights of Hollywood
and Vine. *The future's mine.* She'll build you a railroad.
Collapse the continent to one gone point. Mississippi-Pacific;
teach your children words you've never heard. She'll feed
you peaches swaddled in sweet syrup. *Hurry.* She's a floating
castle, that old crushed dream of monarchy—with democratic
thighs. She's buck-and-rail, pick-axe, wagon wheel. The star
of empire burning at her brow. She'll show you how.
She'll give you everything your rucksack mind desires:
Sharps rifles, hills of bison, the past with its head stuck through
a pillory of bones. She knows you'll let her lead you
when she whispers *Follow.* You'll leave everything you know;
you'll say you're home.

Buffalo Bill's Wild West

To live in hearts we leave behind is not to die.
WILLIAM WIRT WINCHESTER'S EPITAPH

I have knocked the impossible stiff and cold on more than one occasion. I never lost heart.
BUFFALO BILL

Easy for the living to say; easy
for the man with the gun.

The man with long ringlets
worn *for the benefit of any Indian*
who could take my scalp—

each curl a testament to faith
he'd never lose his head. The impossible
shot spinning, dazzling, to the ground

like coins from his daughters' hands
(less easy for his wife
to watch her girls in his rifle's sight:

pretty as sky—with sun-glint
clenched in their fingers). Easy to sell
this show-biz truth: a man who'd killed

4,000 buffalo one dust-skinned year;
who bullwhacked; drove a stagecoach;
won another man's name;

who took the Russian Grand Duke hunting
with the Sioux (wagons clinking
full of caviar behind them). He sailed real Indians

in real teepees to England so the Queen
could see. Easy to amaze: these faces.
These beating hearts. Easy not to ask:

what must be carried inside?
Once, he said, *I crippled a bear, and Mr. Bear*
made for me, charging, but before he reached me,

I had eleven bullets inside him, a little more
lead than he could comfortably digest.
Easy to admire his father—a Quaker—

stabbed for preaching abolition;
his only son, dead young of scarlet fever.
To believe they weighted his heart

so he could not lose it. To need
his wild bullseye faith: the point between
daughter and coin, real-life and show,

where even risking everything comes easy.

Ammunition: Or Sarah Winchester, 23 Years Dead, and My Grandmother, Newly Widowed, Speak

The men were paid extra: danger money.
No metal buttons on their clothes, no cigarettes,

> *In his letters from the South Pacific, he always*
> *called me Honey, made me promise not to forget*

no matches. No hairpins for the women—
So many precautions: fire brigades waiting,

> *to smile for him in the beveled mirror*
> *he'd bought that Christmas—home on leave—*

deep wells, until there were hydrants.
Around the factories, even the horses wore

> *bells everywhere like the sound of ice cracking*
> *when he drove the lake. I'd hold my door open—*

brass instead of steel underfoot. Less chance
of sparks. The men worked overtime—

> *frightened. The months he was gone were*
> *like that. The children in the back of the car,*

gearing up for each new war, or maybe
war. Their shirts couldn't have pockets.

> *holding the shells he'd sent them: speckled around*
> *a tiny curve of breath. Until the telegram,*

No stray bits of metal. And still—each year—
explosions, fires spreading until

> *I kept my promise: smiled as if he could see*
> *my reflection in the bevel of the South Pacific.*

they couldn't count the bodies.

Before his ship was only splinters, smoke

As a child, I thought guncotton sounded

soft—like the cloth for a veil.

Safe As Houses

Do you see how the god always hurls his bolts at the greatest houses and the tallest trees.
HERODOTUS

You want to teach us to be humble, Father
of History—to build ourselves bending
like the house's ice-warped boards. But winters
are long here, the one bare tree painted in
for perspective: how much more alone
we could be. The brushwork of branches

all between us and the sky, which branches
toward dusk: lilac and fragile, an Easter egg farther
than our child-hands. We weather cold alone.
We weather spring's not-coming, the bending
weight of ice, the hail waiting hard in
the clouds. We survive each winter

with patience and nails: the house's winter-
grey boards scabbing after the branches'
scrape. The ice recurs like my mother's dream in
those first years after his death: her father
in his long wool coat, bending
in wind she could not feel. He walked alone

and fast across the fields; she ran alone
behind him, the distance between them—like winter
shadows—lengthening. How could she bend
to a god who hurls ammunition, lightning branching
against our rough-housed love? Dear Father
of History, she believed only in

time. Doing what we have to: folding in
the deadly silk of parachutes (a later war), alone
in her thoughts at that long table: her father
safe inside each fold, or dead. The winter
outside going on. She taught me how fate branches:
one wrong crease could kill. That fabric bending

and smooth as uncrossable fields—bending
as words in our histories. *Safe*—as in
certain. He is safe enough for being hanged. Branches
of gallows. Branches of hope. We face them alone
in our minds. *It's safe to thunder* this winter.
And only later, *safe as a mouse, a house.* Father

of History, our stories begin in winter:
a house and a tree and a god bending branches
of fire. Father of Lies, remind us we are not alone.

The Feet of Ghosts

The ancient notion about spirits of evil was that they were always lame . . .
But modern spiritualists, who supposedly know more than the ancients,
don't seem to think the feet of ghosts are particularly important.
    THE AMERICAN WEEKLY, 1928

[handwritten: Italian Quatrains]

Some nights, my fears come trussed up in red
stilettos: rhinestones and bows like Valentines
and 1981. Like Christmas crackers, mirrors and lines
of coke that once—everyone knocking, knocking—my friend said

We're rock stars, which meant we weren't. Everything shone
just long enough to seem darker: twenty-five
and the dead still far enough away to almost be alive:
my grandfather in aviator goggles, Aunt Judy, Aunt Joan,

not really aunts but my mother's friends who wore
wigs and slippers, or sensible shoes that didn't clack
like my tap teacher's perfect feet. *Heel, toe, ball. Heel, toe, back*
back back. Even as a child, the music was off, or

I was: my body not fishnet and grace, but something caught,
like Cinderella's heel in the stairs as she ran on barefoot,
half-princess, half-loss. Some nights, the past wears one black boot:
Doc Marten, tightly laced, from the pair I bought

in London to dance til dawn while my mother died—
the dancing electric and eccentric, the Good Ship Lollipop
long sunk, but me still wanting to be those women on top
of tables, chairs, stairs in the cabarets, ankles buckled to light.

Command Performance

Armed Forces Radio Network, 1942–49

The soldiers could ask for any sound:
roosters in their Indiana hometowns

crowing at dawn; an operetta; a jive
show with pretty girls, flushed and live-

wired to those notes, jitterbugging
on an old wood floor; Joe Louis slugging

Max Schmeling with his perfect fists;
Dick Tracy in B Flat; the clanking wish

of a jackpot on a nickel slot machine.
Inside the radio's soft static, every dream

served up: the distant sizzle and scorch
of Lana Turner frying a steak—a torch

sputtering above the tiki hut where Lime
and Coca-Cola (and its censored rum)

lilted from the Andrews Sisters' throats;
anything but the night-raid calls: lifeboats,

torpedoes, fire. Jack Benny. Count Basie.
Ann Miller tap dancing fast and racy

in military boots. Tess Trueheart still not
married to Dick Tracy. Charles Laughton

teaching perfect elocution to Donald Duck.
Laughter. Bob Hope. Bing Crosby. Luck.

Transcontinental   *Manifest Destiny*

In a railroad to the Pacific we have a great national work, transcending,
in its magnitude, and in its results, anything yet attempted by man.
AMERICAN RAILROAD JOURNAL

Gunpowder and Chinamen were the only weapons . . . builders had
with which to fight the earth and stone through which they had to pass, laid
in their path centuries ago by the Creator.
ENGINEER FOR THE TRANSCONTINENTAL RAILROAD

I. Crazy Judah (1859)

They said he might as well build a railroad
to the moon, his maps laid out like lakes
in the desert. *What is needed is a proper survey.*
His maps laid out like a whorehouse Bible.
Who would touch it? Who believed a man
who made a mountain range a molehill,
who tunneled and gun-powdered granite
fact to lay his tracks *out of the ruck of things?*
Who promised tightrope-narrow ridges
holding trains—not years from now, but
now. *What's needed are the men and money,*

not just plans. Who charted routes across
the Long Ravine and Donner Pass where
fear split open: black oak in a lightning
storm, where rivers spilled like thought
too fast to follow. His wife said, *You're giving*
away your thunder. He said, *This country is*
a house divided. Who would join it? With
what hammers and stakes could men cross
a continent he had to sail around to say,
There is another way. It is a well-known maxim:
The gods wait for a beginning before they lend their aid.

II. The Big Four (1862)

Because they were men of vision,
which meant men of money, believers
in the Northern route to the new free West,
believers in the pocket-creased maps

of surveyors, the bare-armed muscles
of strangers, the sledgehammer strikes,
the new flanged rails, the country healed
in its iron lung—they invested funds

to sail from the Eastern seaboard and
around Cape Horn: shiploads of crowbars,
hammers, dump carts, rails, switches,
spikes, tents, hitches, plows, drills,

everything but camels (the Confederate
plan to cross the Southern desert):
the country an infinite snake: mouth
gaping around the future's iron tail.

III. The Workers (1866)

The records admit *no record of the hands*
and fingers lost in the blasting: the grand

and everyday explosions of granite into light,
the times they tried to hide in time

but couldn't (something in the way: a horse,
loose rubble, exhaustion). Or the loss

from sledgehammers. Eighteen pounds rising,
striking, rising. The first heat of day slicing

cold muscles—that swinging til only opium
could hold them still for sleep—the pig-iron

snow-plow pushing even then through
dreams—splitting continents, families, youth

into heaps beside it, or the train steaming off
its tracks through their bones: their coughs

like nails in tamarack trusses, their ribs
full of gunpowder, as outside the *iron ribbon,*

as history would call it, shone. As if
all they were doing was stitching

along the country's seam: shimmery, simple,
whatever fingers they had safe in thimbles.

IV. The Sierras (1867)

Already dead of yellow fever years before,
Judah never saw two thousand men from China
work for weeks inside those long white tents
of snow: the tunnels they lived inside, ate inside,

blasted, and tunneled further, the walls
they hard-packed against gravity, the dank smoke-
haze and fear of falling sky in which they learned
to move like snow itself: a stiff suspension,

particulate, a joined numbness. Only the steam
of tea, a bit of corn meal. Talk of eating
the horses. Silence for days after the avalanche,
a weighted quiet like every white key

on a piano played at once, then never played.
The survivors working faster now: black powder,
rails, reed-thatched baskets, in which, when spring
came, they would dangle over chasms—afraid

of the air now—blinking in the rain-bleached light:
the river below gleaming like another railroad
built while they burrowed: all rushing wheels—
what the dead, when they thawed, would ride.

V. Sherman's Peace Council with the Indians (1867)

We
built
iron
roads
and
you
cannot
stop
the
locomotive
any
more
than
you
can
stop
the
sun
or
moon.

VI: Ferguson's Diary (1868)

And then we passed through a dismal
and desolate country: a terrible country:
all sage brush and grease weed and the mules
out of their depth in the river, swiftly
carried by currents: the awful look of terror

and despair as two men went down. My level
tangled in the wagon box, so I had to drop
it or be dragged under. I never found it
or the guns or men we'd lost. No matter

the death toll, the engineers are concerned
with the bridge and making some money.

Some Indians made a dash on some pilgrims
at sunrise. Later we were attacked by Indians
and succeeded in shooting one. Four men
were killed and scalped. I have no sympathy

for the red devils. May their dwelling places
and habitations be destroyed. May the greedy
crows hover over their silent corpses.

Two men were shot this evening
in a drunken row. Another man and four
mules drowned. A man was wounded, another
killed: occasioned by some personal difficulty.

The carelessness and reckless disregard
for life and limb, the promiscuous shooting
is perfectly outrageous and alarming.

Still, the bridge is a success.

The first passenger train crossed
the ridge at noon. The time is coming

and fast, too, when
there will be no West.

VII. Hell-on-Wheels (1868)

Hell, one foreman said, must have been raked
to furnish them: these men and women

who rolled from field to field: the buildings slap-
dash built: canvas and shanties: the Germania House

with its whiskey and 50-cent meals, its hurdy-gurdy
dancing: skirts hiked up to God-Knows:

and the rail crews' hungers sledgehammer heavy:
lanterns and legs and the hip bones of strangers:

a few slung-down hours: something stronger
than iron: Benton, Laramie, Bear River City,

Corrine: *which is fast becoming civilized—several men
having been killed there already:* the alkali dust

ankle-deep and shifty as gunpowder: the men
white as roaches in a barrel of flour: the women

powdered sweet over filth: the one bookstore
(in one photograph) maybe a joke: a den

of antiquity: the broken spines, loose pages
caught in these crosswinds like the cottonwood

where Dugan—hands cuffed by vigilantes—
had begged to leave the country, *and he did,*

*when the rope pulled taut, and the wagon drove
away:* the corpse of Damocles dangling

over scrub weed: the trains unloading
their own future rails: a bitch birthing whelps

in the dust: bones under bourbon floorboards:
it was monstrous, wondrous, hideous inside those tents

and buildings: transitory as soap bubbles:
rainbows and scum.

VIII. Jack Morrow and Friends (1868)

    after the photograph by Arundel Hull

After Hull climbs his camera down from the windmill—half-built,
rickety as light on this dust-storm morning—
after he climbs down from a boxcar—the station sleeping
in the drunk dawn—the barrels of gunpowder Morrow stole
from his own wagon trains emptied (for later sale), then filled with sand
to sell to strangers: this moment: Morrow seated on a barrel, long legs
draped over the hoop, pin-striped, casual, palms against thighs, his elbows
jutted out to show he knows his body's value: twice the space
of other men's. His posse—even the man in front—a backdrop: creased-up
brims and crumpled suits and watch-fobs shining in this flat light
that is not about shining, but staring straight like the man who chose
not to steal this camera when he robbed Hull's stage. Who can
perform at will the miracle of gunpowder into sand into money
into (short-counted) ties to sell the railroad. Who lights his cigars
from burning bank notes while the workers wait.

IX: *Roving Delia Fish Dance* (1869)

This telegrammed challenge from Hopkins to Huntington
which meant, decoded: *We're laying track at a rate of 4 miles
every day.* The U.P. pioneers with their shovels at dawn
aligning the night-laid ties as more men moved behind:
pairs with tongs to lift the rails, position them, drop
them. Position them, drop them. The foreman calling
Down! The fields tamped and graded for their iron crop—
U.P. to C.P., C.P. to U.P.—that must outrace its own growing.
The trains caught in snowstorms. Stalling. The papers
calling the Union Pacific *an elongated human slaughterhouse.*
The foreman calling out *Down!* The papers asking *Where
and when will they ever be joined? ROVING DELIA FISH-
DANCE.* We are working as fast as is human—headlong
as slick fish. We are dancing with sledgehammers, tongs.

X: The Golden Spike, Promontory, Utah (May 10, 1869)

Even then—noise, confusion,
crowding. The reporters
couldn't see. History says
Hewes (a baron of sand dunes)
presented it. *13 ounces approximate
gold.* No sledge marks to show
if it was struck at all—if Stanford
missed, as they say. No marks
from removal. Laurel and gold.
As if the railroad had always been
a simple shining. *What's needed
are the men and money.* A simple
striking, like luck in a pan.
What's needed is a proper survey.
The country laid out like a map
of itself: a whorehouse Bible,
a house united. Judah's
widow (by coincidence,
their anniversary) not invited.
I refused myself to everyone that day.
Those two trains waiting to inch
nose to nose: The No. 119,
The Jupiter. Smash of champagne
(or wine) against the cattle catchers,
strike of blows (or silence
of the silver maul's misses).
That spike bristling like an oak
in lightning. The live wires flashing
that one bright signal
coast-unto-coast. *It is done.*
(Not years from now, but now.)
Cannon fire in Salt Lake City,
D.C., San Francisco. That spike:
a single rail to the sun.

Port of Oakland

As the recession lengthened, the freeway grew
louder, as though everyone drove now
instead of working: a pitch map of engines droning
and whining past our block, semis shirring
and shifting down into our sleep. We traded stress
dreams: a shark fighting a zebra. A stadium of students
facing away. Blood in the waves. Omens or the rush
of strangers' tires? Dark. Incessant. The lists. The push
of rain against our leaning chimney. What we needed
to fix, or leave, or try to love. Sometimes, we fled
to watch container ships unloading vast, identical
boxes stamped *Hanjin*. We could pretend they held
anything we wanted. Mysterious, sealed
like the paper fortune tellers we used to fold
as children: names of boys, cities, cars, jobs
secreted in triangles. Each future different. Rob.
Brian. London. Paris. Porsche. Doctor. Pirates had come
back in the news. Kids from Africa stealing guns
and ships. Blackmarket cargo. At first, it sounded unreal:
like dragons lifting goats from the city, or banshees'
seagull screech. We drank wine at the top
of the lookout tower until the night cops,
locking up, asked what we were doing. Waiting
for the future. *Hanjin. Hanjin. Hanjin. Hanjin.*

L.C. Smith and Bros., Makers of Fine Guns and Typewriters, Advertise

With the same sweep—one, two, or three lines

so handsome in engraving, embellishment, and finish

makes all-day speed easy for the operator

you will be delighted to the point of ecstasy

a combined one-motion carriage return and line space

insures the hunter good sport

no lost time, no wasted energy, no mistakes or misplaced letters

the proper aim is up to you, but you can leave the results to us

the inexorable law of Survival of the Fittest is proved

take it with you and give yourself a fair chance

ball bearing, long wearing, hair trigger

improvements cease to stand out against the background of "No Shortcomings"

a necessity for emphasizing

the fullest possible pleasure in the field, and the maximum game in your bag

no necessary operation takes the hands from writing position

prevents fumbling and delay

a key for every character

it speaks with a directness and force

which leaves no room for doubt as to its meaning

Barbed Wire Bible

In the beginning: grindstones and glinting
cursive. A thousand patterns to twine

the same wire. The Zig-Zag, The Spur,
The Telegraph Splice, The Kelly Thorny

Common. The preachers railed against
"The Devil's Rope"—the cattle bleeding.

*The Earth is not your Mother; it's the creation
of your Father*, says the pickup barreling

south to Carrizozo. My nephews, raised
in this ghost town, invent the names

of ghosts; one rings the tower bell:
ricochets of silence. *God's powers are neutral,*

*like a zero. By breaking the circle, you can shape
any letter or number.* Hanging Barb. Merrill

Four-Point Twirl. Dodge Six-Point Star.
In what used to be the school—*not only*

an ornament, but an absolute necessity—names
of every child who sat in these knife-nicked

seats. Gabriel, a kid when I last saw him,
gangly and quiet, lifts his shirt: *El que no habla,*

Dios no lo oye. Inside the florid script's pink
Mexican ink, a naked woman. *If you don't speak,*

God won't hear you. My sister says, "I thought
he'd be a scientist or monk." Bet-a-Million

Gates stampeded his longhorns in the new
corral with gunshots and torches—*Light as*

air, cheap as dirt, and strong as good whiskey—
to prove the knots would hold.

Reconstruction

After our house, its thirteen rooms
and one hundred years, burned
to the ground, my mother said
she'd known it would happen.
Her premonitions leaned backwards
like shadows on the timothy grass,
like the chicken coop my parents tore
down when I was young: the facts
of wire and boards pried loose as if
the world were always a hammer's claw
away from disassembly. *I cannot consent,*
wrote Hawthorne, *to have heaven and
earth, this world and the next, beaten
together like the white and yolk of an egg,*
yet he listened often to talk of psychics,
mesmerism, ghosts. The past and future
spilling through the present's cracks,
not flaring once, but smoldering inside
my mother's mind. *I could see it, but
couldn't stop it,* she said. *I didn't want
you to worry.* Fearing suspicions of arson,
she left our paintings to char. An exhibit
of futility and fate. The blueprints
for absence, rolled and waiting as we
drove away. *I am unwilling that such a power
should be exercised on you of which we know
neither origin nor consequence,* he wrote
his fiancé, cured of her headaches
by magnetic powers. *Enthusiasts who adopt
such extravagant ideas appear to me to lack
imagination.* Impossible to know what
my mother had known and what
grief built. Sudden shell of a house
she'd lived in thirty years. The stairs
that led to a landing that led nowhere:
a hanging ledge where in my one
recurring dream, I lived happily
in the ruined air—as if I always had.

Spiritualists' Iniquities Unmasked: Or Kate and Margaret Fox, Accused of Fraudulent Communication with the Dead, Respond, 1860

They say we have been *prostituted*
to this wicked trade; cracking our toes
to summon the figment
of a ghost. As though the dead

were nothing more than bones
in our own bodies—pulled apart.
They say our *wonders are often*
blunders; we do not know

a child's age, a woman's loss
(the facts the living know). The spirits
do not come when called. Silent
as masonry, as moss

on any grave. We don't deny this:
the walls between the worlds,
or the cracks. The thin divide.
The knocks on doors that don't exist

inside our house. The sound pours
like milk through butter muslin,
straining out—who knows?
It's not for us to ask. The wares

the peddler brings are plain:
John Bell once killed him
here and filled in cellar holes
to hide his crime. We claim

only the truth we hear—the raps
and knocks that answer when
we knock. The Unknown Tongues
have chosen us. A demon's trap,

they say in town; we've strayed
from Christ's pure words (but He
rose, too, and rolled the stone aside).
Believe us: we have knelt and prayed,

and standing, been accused that it's
our knees that snap and make
the sounds. Now, Doctor Lee
calls it *Knëeology. Weak and half-witted*

as they say we are, we know
stiff knees from speech, our bodies
from the air. Why should the spirit—
holy as it is—stay boxed in heaven, closed

from all but God? And who should fear—
who has not secrets
grouted in the walls; who has not
traded with the Devil—what we may hear?

Sand Creek Testimony

George Bent, Tsistsistas (Southern Cheyenne) 1864

I heard Black Kettle call the people: *Do not fear;*
the soldiers will not hurt you. He held a large American
flag on a pole at his lodge. Then the troops opened fire—

cannons, rifles—drunken yells of soldiers slicing ears,
scalps, private parts from the bodies of our women.
Some stretched skin like blankets over saddles. *Do not fear*

Greenwood had told us at the treaty signing. *Live here*
on this (1/13th of this) *land we give you. Americans—*
if you raise a flag on a pole—will know to not open fire,

will know that you're peaceful. That day, our best warriors
had ridden west to hunt bison. The brains of our women
knocked out with rocks, children wailing in fear

as cannon fire surged and thundered floods over
our fields. These were Chivington's orders. Americans,
yes, lifted fetuses, genitalia like flags in that fire;

they murdered without reason or warning—here
on the land we were promised. They cut women
to strips like red stripes on that flag that calls fear
to all hearts now—waving as the troops opened fire.

Elizabeth "Plinky" Topperwein, Champion Markswoman, Remembers

My husband never missed a playing
      card's thin edge; could ride a bicycle while
throwing balls he'd shoot straight through—
      impressive, yes, but from the sidelines
like any circus trick—the lions yawning
      at their trainers' whips—his hands,
afterwards, numb when he touched me.
      I wanted to understand the sky
he aimed into—not empty air, or blue
      or gun-smoke scrim, but a target
clearer than home; a constellation of clay
      and gun and bullet's light he saw
in that instant of its making and unmaking.

Was that the instant of my making or unmaking?
      The first clay disk plinked down, another
thrown, and me, the girl who'd only handled
      guns on factory lines, become one finger
squeezing back, one eye, one exhalation held
      until the shot let go. It wasn't sky at all
but earth I saw—dust waiting to be dust,
      like all of us. I let it be. I let the clay
break open, wishbone snapped and blown
      back to itself. No purled stitch or bed
of sweet green peas, but Eve's own work—
      to take the knowledge as she saw it:
target-bright, waiting against dark leaves for her.

Target-bright against dark leaves outside
      the gun pavilion at the World's Fair:
those glass balls—amber, ridged—1,000
      launched, 967 hit. A record, though Ad
bested that: missed only 4 of 50,000 blocks:
      wood splintering so deep he dreamed
for nights of blocks a mile away, the bullets
      stuck. He'd wake with knotted arms

to shoot again—a lighted match extinguished
        between fingertips, mirror sighting,
backwards, lying down. I knew it wasn't
        prizes he was after then but sound
to stop the awful silence of his sleep.

He'd found me in an awful, silent sleep:
        those hours loading ammunition
on the line; each Winchester the same
        to me: barrel, trigger, stock.
Guns are like men, I learned, you never
        know them til they speak. He was
a missionary back from touting rifles
        in the West, a gunsmith's son
with circus tricks. I knew because the girls
        whispered this. He only said
I'm Adolph Topperwein, and you're Elizabeth.
        He stood there, steady, watching
as the future broke in pieces at my feet.

The future kept breaking daily at our feet—
        the train tracks first; then all the birds
turned clay as if God made the world
        hollow for our sport. The gun so hot
sometimes they'd pour ice water
        over like a fevered child. We couldn't
stop. It was our job. Those wings made
        platen for the blast, and shoulders,
sore, and Ad shooting each day for weeks
        and Annie Oakley calling *me*
the sharpest woman shot. Pride goes before
        the fall, they say, but it wasn't
pride. It was my job to tell the gun's straight truth.

2,000 times I had to tell the gun's straight truth
        that day—the pigeons skimmed
so fast they seemed one speck suspended,
        hands so raw by noon I couldn't feel,
only brace against exhaustion's ricochet.
        The blistering took my palm like
snakeskin off. I wondered if I might grow back
        some other life. I'd once been fortune-
told my lines arced high away from home. I missed
        it, yes, but went where competition called:
those Marlins, Remingtons, and us. Lucky
        we both could shoot, lucky to lie at night—
our bodies just human then, willing to be weak.

My body was human then, willing to be weak
        as I bore him, blood and fist and wail.
He was more warmth than weight, a scrap
        of some soft core inside I'd never see.
I had to learn that softness pressed against
        a shoulder used to wood. His face
so tentative, so like our own it frightened me.
        Already, he was less surely mine
than any shot, and also mine—a moment
        of light split open from the barrel
of this flesh. What are any of us beyond
        this? Our lives lined up like edgewise
playing cards we aim at, praying not to miss.

Many a Goat

The imitative faculties of the . . . boy and his desire for glory
have been greatly stimulated by the coming of Buffalo Bill's Wild West Show.
Many a peaceful dog has been roped . . . by urchins whose imagination
converted him into a bucking bronco; many a goat has been mistaken
for a rampant buffalo and hunted over imaginary Rocky Mountains.
    BROOKLYN EAGLE, 1894

A rowdy teenager named René Secrétan, who liked to dress up in a cowboy
costume he'd bought after seeing Buffalo Bill's Wild West show, was probably
the source of the gun.
    NEW YORK TIMES BOOK REVIEW, VAN GOGH—THE LIFE, 2011

Even here in Auvers, the boys are not immune
to the West's wild lure. They buy drinks for Van Gogh—
send their girlfriends to taunt with false
seductions. Pretty peasants, innocent prostitutes:
the imagination turns cotton to silk, cornflower blue
into the red-striped candy of garters; farmyards into Hell-
on-Wheels towns that roll behind rail crews
like a dark flock of crows. Van Gogh understands this:
mountains spiring through cornstalks,
snow capping the summer fields: lead-white
in a swirl of sunflowers. Many a peaceful dog
would rather be a bronco. Many a boy,
a canvas. Broken sky. The meringue of prairie schooners.
The imaginary plains where guns gleam, pistol-twirled
stars above cypress. Many a tree
would rather be a church steeple. Many a church steeple:
fire's scorch and gutter through the thatches
of men's hearts. Maybe it's true he steals
the pistol—antique, likely to malfunction—
holds it angle-askew in the field: a brush to swathe
the wound of a body. Maybe it's true
the boys aim it. Their Dutch-Indian enemy, innocent,
inebriated: Yellow Bonnet's war paint and canvas: lodge poles
of madness holding up his mind. They've seen it all
before: blood on stage, and Bill himself,
that scalp in his upraised fingers like a palette,

a sun-spot, a gold-glass bottle. Van Gogh
understands this. He is not the first man
for whom death is beautiful.

Widowed

After awhile, she looked like any desert
woman: long horse-line of jaw, blue eyes, more sky
than lake. In the sand-swept yard, she steeped sun
tea in gallon jars—the days marked by its colors:
gold-brown swirls skeining loose like blood
into water. More rust than sunset. Earth
troweled up by Adirondack lakes: loam
and soft rotting wood. She dreamed about
winter: maple sap tapped into buckets,
boiled and drizzled over snow. Stretching
and sweet. The tea turned the color of early fall
leaves; the tea turned the color of her hair,
unpinned now—her mother-in-law, a ghost note
in her mind: *proper women don't wear their hair
down. Proper, married women.* The tea let its dark
strands loose. Tarantula brown. Tanned leather.
The taste: dry and acrid. The taste: scorched.
Sugarless. Desert filling the jar's curved glass.

My Mother Reads to Her Daughters: *Great Expectations*

AND if we found someone who loved us—stable
(with stables), velvet-suited (well-suited)—found

ourselves dressing for the altar, white pearl
buttons down our back, our skin rose-watered, lost

inside lace. BUT we didn't keep him, dropped
him as girls are always dropping doll shoes—found

only when the dolls are gone. IF we put him somewhere
safe but then forgot—cherry red barrettes lost

in a lunch box. If we let him forget us. If we
didn't dazzle in handmade dresses, coats found

at thrift-stores. If we didn't roll with the punches.
IF we stood there in the aisle—lace-stunned, lost

as a child in a snowstorm. Those unforgiving flowers,
ice-white, cake-white, white so thick we only found

our way by turning, running: all those faces watching
our religion raveling. WE'D wear only the lost

shreds of our beauty. We'd sit cordoned in the dust-
caked banquet; curtained so no sun could find

our faces. We would frighten whoever found
us—there between the pages of old heartbreak—
moldering, never married to anything but loss.

Stereoscope: California

The concentration of the whole attention ... produce[s] a ... kind of clairvoyance, in which we seem to leave the body behind us and sail away into one strange scene after another, like disembodied spirits.
OLIVER WENDELL HOLMES

How else can we enter history
as it is: the ladies' downcast eyes
before the Devil's Pulpit: a geyser
spuming in the woods behind them,
slender as their walking sticks;
the earth mouthing its apocalypse
as they hold their hat brims proper
in their hands. They are posing
to prove they are here. Their bodies
drifting into shadowed focus
for the lenses—as we are drifting
to the Hotel del Monte, turreted
and balconied, a new scene where we're
climbing from a carriage, its wheels
so round and real we nearly stumble
startled by the fullness of the world,

Even now, it's beginning to appear:
glass plates in collodion, the dark
separating from the light, rising—
redwoods taller than the frame,
an acorn cache, cedar thatched,
for the bone-grinding winters;
tourists posing with native baskets
by the sweat house, river-logged,
where the hunters come to bathe
to lose their human scent, be woods,
things without names. Shapes shift
like dunes against ocean: pale grey
in the negative box: the world still
breakable—some destiny developing
out of grass and sand and people
brought into a single image, blurred,

its Lotta-Crabtree curves. She's gold
rush and bustle and a smile inside
that hint of smile; our private peep-
show, and we're just eyes until we are
not pairs of eyes, but space we too can
rest in. Ocean Beach swept smooth
by wind, the sky cloudless as always,
the men's black suits in dark relief
against the haze of grey. The waves
of parasols, smooth moon-white
like Half Dome, split from a
once-doubled, irretrievable self—

in the pan, then everything clear—
the darkroom tent folding into itself,
show for the tourists and necessity's
invention. These portable darknesses
fill with faces we keep hoping to
like—a blank slate or our history
written in a silver bath, still drying.
The camera crouched like a spider
on stiff legs reminding us this game
is waiting: catching what we can,
more ancient rock or sky, hoping this
will help us see to some better place.

The Door to Nowhere

is, from the inside, locked and ordinary
so the little girl on the tour who keeps
asking in each room if we're there yet
has to be prodded by her mother—look:

the guide already cheerfully spieling off
deaths and rumors and yards of antique
wallpaper—Lincrusta, imported—glass
valued at $25,000, spider webs that held

some significance for Mrs. Winchester,
although no one knows what—Ariadne
with her fleece of facts we trail room to
room, the little girl clearly disappointed,

twisting glances back at the blank brown
unfinished wood, for the first time maybe
fearing how boring nowhere might be—
exactly like somewhere invented by adults,

like the back of her closet that never opens
to Narnia, although she sits on her shoes,
scrunched in the dark, and waits—hoping
with her whole body even now her mother

is wrong, and there's another door coming
to that darker-than-Space-Mountain space
where all of us might dissolve if we went,
but we wouldn't, only her, who's truly—

wherever we won't let her go—not afraid

Ghost Tours: Houdini

Each year, at his death-day séance,
he did not appear: the room full
of the space where he wasn't,
as once the air had been: his body
upside down in the Upside Down,
its glass bright with water—
no bubbles, no struggle, just twisting

his wrists free his arms his ankles,
a trick like all tricks. He'd promised
he wouldn't return. He knew
the body's limits: how it could wrestle
out of ropes, chains, locks, metal
milk cans, the bat-hung building pose.
But death was no straightjacket, no

steamer trunk clicked shut for
the Metamorphosis. No knot tied
looser than a living muscle's pull. It didn't
applaud as you jumped—bound—
from the bridge. No one returned.

And the medium's proofs—a cross
his Jewish mother drew, his name
in English (a language she never
spoke): the cheapest stunts. Hope
for the ones who never dared turn
headfirst from the seventh floor
to see the crowd below—eyes

raised up as if for God, but more
than God. A human strung from
his ankles and unafraid. Watch
closely: this is how the living
know they live; how freedom
must come before breath. Watch
closer: this is all there is.

John Brown, First Proprietor of the Winchester Mystery House, Explains, 1926

I was planning a roller coaster—the Backity Back—
my invention. The tracks leading forward to tracks
that led back. The way thinking carries us, then whips
us. The way maybe she built this: each morning's trip
down new stairs leading back up old stairs. Not death
but the fear that precedes—the long rickety climb, yes,
that clacking, then the quiet at the peak when we know.

Sure, I never finished building; I was waiting, you know,
for more cash—spun like cotton-candy from fear: yes
they all wanted thrills. I sold tours of hallways to death,
slipped in cordite and ghosts. The truth's just one trip,
and we always want more: earthquakes that whip
off whole towers like hats. You can't tell from the tracks,
won't know til it hits you: that ride on the Backity Back.

Calamity Jane, Somewhat Inebriated, Thinks of Writing to Oliver Winchester

Sure, the guns are good, but it's your shirts
I liked the best: the ones you used to make
with the necks sewn so they didn't slip—shit,
I'd wear them every day with trousers, take

whatever wife's man. It's not all bang, bang
bang the way they say. There are bodies too
beneath stiff cuffs. Women shouldn't hang
themselves between lace and lady. Yes, its true:

that charge of fornication. Yes, it's true: guns
make a hard life quicker. It's how we wear
ourselves that matters, though. Worn out, done-
for, or doing-in. If you came through here,

I'd drink your shirt off, Button. It's your loss.
Holes are free; it's cloth and bone that costs.

Ghost Tours: Diamond Bessie, 1877

It wasn't just the jewels; the couple
had all their own teeth, and arrived

by train with matching luggage—her
glittering around the Capitol Hotel,

and him packing the picnic lunch.
They sat on the red velvet couch still

in the lobby, and no one knew his real
name, or that his family in Europe

kept zebras to pull their coaches—not
til later at the trial. The ants had found

the bullet hole in her head and circled
it like honey. A well-dressed corpse.

Though she was a prostitute, really—
a *dues-paying soiled dove*. He was caught

in Cincinnati, convicted, acquitted. Shot
one eye out attempting suicide. *A crime*

unparalleled in the record of blood. Texas' first
big murder. Two days he waited to leave

Jefferson: wore her rings to breakfast,
with her sprawled there by the basket—

like he wanted someone to guess she
wasn't visiting friends in the bayou,

or was hoping she'd wake—yawning
and rubbing her eyes at the light

that must look better than diamonds
if you've been dead for a little while.

How It Happened

Daisies border the lawn
like poor embroidery. You do not want them
to be beautiful. Thick-hearted,

on their wayward stems. No one can explain
why you deserve this. Not the doctor. Not
the clock. Not God

in his stained-glass field. The flood recedes.
The fire swerves around your house, your bed, your
face. Hard roses on the breakfast china.

Everyone at their time, they tell you.
The nurse crying in the nursery. The crib
carried down, the buckling

floor. You watch light through the ivy—
day making its same mistakes; spring rain
straying into summer. You breathe as the last

coughs rake blood from his lungs. No one
can change this. The bodies are buried;
music seeps from shutters—hurricane plywood;

cracked glass; the station where the train will leave
in a wake of dumb bright songs. No one can take back
what you prayed. You wanted to live.

You wanted to be safe.

Ghost Tours: Asphodel Plantation, 1975

That inconsolable night, I cried at nothing
my parents could see: the four-poster bed's

mahogany whorls holding up a canopy
of dark, or the doorknob imperceptibly

turning. Something wanted to come in
from the thin dirt roads that led nowhere

the living needed go—moonless fields
where Spanish moss draped all the trees

like tatters of the sky's old elegance, the air
thickened with a churn of voices that were

not voices even when they were: bird calls
of slaves and the will-o-wisps of bodies

skirting death. What could I, at one, have
known of this, or anything? And still I cried

so hard my parents pushed at last the armoire
to the door to ward off something—

worrying then they'd locked something in
instead. Was it their own unspoken fears

I wailed for? The long night road the book
neglected to describe? Peeling wallpaper

in the dining room; the crab claws floating
in the soup? Later, they would describe

these first: the way they rose, or seemed
to still be rising, from the broth, and how

the waiters, shadows on the walls, looked on.
Eyes empty as the spoons my parents held.

Sarah Winchester, 23 Years Dead, Goes to the Movies: *House of Dracula*

(in which Dracula, The Wolf Man, and Frankenstein's Monster arrive at Dr. Edelman's house for treatment)

Is it safer when all the monsters gather
inside one house: one place to summon

and fear? The sweep of the Count's black
wing—a premonition at the doctor's door,

who answers, of course, who lets him in,
takes him down the basement stairs. Wide

as cemetery gates—the entrance to oblivion.
We don't ask why: the doctor with his shock-

white beard, his coffin full of Transylvanian
soil. Our bodies, too, wait in the dark, wanting

what they cannot want. Must we be given each
some curse? A face that furs and jowls at rising

moons? A body patchworked out of death?
In his greenhouse, the doctor tends rare molds

to reshape brains: the skull bones pliant as
music. We watch the Wolf change back into

a changeless man. He loves the nurse now:
her moonbeam white dresses. But Dracula

wants her, makes her play piano jazz riffs—
staccato, more staccato—with his eyes.

Despite ourselves, we understand that pull:
bone keys at midnight waiting for our hands,

the spirits waiting. Now even the doctor's mad:
vampiric-blooded, stopping at nothing. What

cure remains? The house in flames. Everyone
so monstrous, so human.

Sarah Winchester Reads *Great Expectations*

Of course you miss him, but it's worse to waste
a lifetime eating from a cobwebbed plate—
A moth caught in a white lace snare: the future
growing brittle as old icing. Fleur-de-lis and sugar
roses swirling like a waltz without the orchestra.
If love doesn't jilt you, death will leave you china-
cracked and kneeling in the orchard's empty aisles,
the plums decked out like bridesmaids for the sky
or grievers ripening back to joy. You'll be alone
too young. You'll need the veil like a gravestone:
a way to bury who you were: the naïve girl who
thought her house was built. Better to draw new
rooms he's never lived in, staircases to any place
he maybe is. Count nails; forget the crumbled cake.

B. Tyler Henry

Gunsmith, Master Mechanic, and Inventor of *The Most Effective Weapon in the World,* 1860

Sewing machines were always temporary—slack
drive belts and lithium grease on gears, and women
whirring around me like wasps in nests of cloth.
I missed the guns. How, almost-human, they pushed back,

recoiled or refused to fire. I missed their faithful dark:
the cartridges waiting inside the magazine as souls
must do somewhere before this earth, and after. Breech
and lever, those rimfires rushed fresh through—the art

of shot-followed shot. My hands understood before
the metal could; my hands—before Winchester's own—
fired the *ne plus ultra,* as they're calling it, of Repeating
or Revolving Arms. The firing pin, the bolt, the lore

of new-flanged cartridges and sixteen shots, I'd trade
for nothing. I saw this: willing, ready to be made.

Whole Cloth

If her wealth had derived from something other than a firearm—
a sewing machine, for example . . . no one would have suggested
she feared . . . ghosts of garment workers.
MARY JO IGNOFFO, SARAH WINCHESTER BIOGRAPHER

I wish I had invented a lawnmower.
MIKHAIL KALASHNIKOV, AK 47 INVENTOR

Somewhere, there is a backstitch on our lives—
the seams sewn firm, the needle precise

and forgiving. We pull the cord, and the motor
will always wake. Inside the house, the bobbin whirs

as our mother hems; the iron-steam singe
of summer in rooms we'll go on living in.

There is no fire, only the sweet, cut grass
and gasoline. The roaring doubling back,

receding. The world is being made of dust
and gabardine and pins. It is enough

to keep the ghosts away. They are buttons
in their perfect holes. We are tended lawns,

the permanent cavity made impermanent
and healed. Somewhere, we learn to invent

only beauty—a swath of green, a collar
smooth at our necks. At the end, only the blur

of years without regrets; those benevolent blades;
our lives spooling free of their threads.

Bison Bison

In 1890, a distinct bison cow and one bison bull were transported
from the rolling Great Plains to the urban paradise of
the Golden Gate Park. The cow was named Sarah Bernhardt,
while the bull was called Ben Harrison. The Park Commission
beamed with pride as such possessions roamed about their land.
   "BUFFALO IN GOLDEN GATE PARK"

Already, almost *a majestic memory,* those 2 of 1,000
survivors: those walking rugs that grazed
this paddock first: curious and grand

as Bernhardt's lies. She was not yet the Divine
Sarah, not yet Hamlet: travesty minstrel, mistress,
courtesan (after convent school), actress

who slept in a coffin. It helped—she said—
to understand her tragic roles, as the train ride
must have helped the bison understand the instability

of land, its greased and wheeled tendency
to roll: 30 million ancestors in a single century
turned from living beasts to the drive belts

in factories. *By destroying the buffalo, we destroy*
the Indian's food. No tragic soliloquies. Just
staging. Sometimes history is simple:

the bland-eyed president, a wooly bull
munching grass served up from sand dunes.
In the White House—the first electric lights,

and rumors: Harrison and his wife too scared
to touch the switches. Inveterate showman, hired
gun for the railroad, Buffalo Bill wrote, *We'd ride*

ten or twelve days through solid herds. Skulls
piled tall as steam trains: thick hides for miles
rotting in the prairie sun. If no lover came,

she'd sleep all night in that coffin. If no
servant came, they'd sleep all night
with the lights on. Ladies in lace dresses—

taking ocean air—would gawk at these new
old creatures, asleep standing upright: rumpled
as stage sets from a traveling show.

The General Store Proprietor

What did it matter why she built? She paid in gold.
She took her time rejecting bolts of taffeta, inspecting
brocatelle in the dim carriage light. I've never sold
cloth like that again. She'd buy all we had of anything
she liked. Brocade. Cretonne. Our business was to spool
and unspool. Moreen. Serge. Saxony. They said she had
two carpenters dismissed for seeing her without her veil
(she ordered tulle). I never saw her either—just her hands
in black silk buttoned to the wrist. The drapes' velvet
would lift less than a gust of wind. She had good taste.
What did it matter if she rang strange bells or met
the dead? For thirty years, I sold her arrasene and lace,
the finest fabric San Jose has known. Perhaps
she wanted new windows to dress. I never asked.

Winchester .351 High-Power Self-Loading Rifle

It was the love which the hunter has for living things,
and which he can only express by aiming his gun at them.
ITALO CALVINO

Who doesn't dream of a heart *with all sights*
attached, all moving parts enclosed? A love
that *can shoot through steel?* See how the cougar eyes
the bold word *Winchester*—its jagged rush—

his body, whisker-close against the cliff, unflinching.
Already he's prey: his muscled legs like roots
too deep for springing; a pendulum stilling
for the chime of fate. Who wouldn't lose

this skin for an instant of lightning—one
flash from *the lightest, strongest, handsomest*
repeater ever made? Who hasn't gone
to a ledge like this and waited? The scent

on the wind that draws them: lover or devil,
the heart reloading even as it recoils.

The Blueprint

Because the prophecy said *build*: this room
hinged to sky, a doorway, a sill, a step, a floor,
a chimney with nothing to burn. The ghosts
have brick-dust on their clothes, gun-powder
bones. All night, the hammers christen wood:
railings, spindles, joists, baseboards, cupboards
in cupboards, frames, posts, hallways; the only way
to life, this labyrinth. A window to a window.
Trapdoor. Skylight. Stairway, each small step
eternally divided. The ghosts have sawdust
in their hair. Demolished wings. New sketches
for forgiveness. Ballroom. Bedroom. Cupola.
Carriage house. Walls around every emptiness.

Notes on the Poems

Sarah Winchester (1839–1922) was the widow of William Wirt Winchester, son of Oliver Winchester, owner of the Winchester Repeating Arms Company. According to legend, after William died of tuberculosis in 1881 (which followed their one child, Annie, dying in infancy in 1866), Sarah consulted a Spiritualist medium, who told her to move West and endlessly construct a house to appease (or house) the ghosts of everyone killed with Winchester rifles—since the ghosts were responsible for the deaths of William and Annie, and would kill her next. She was said to hold séances to consult the ghosts about construction. An alternate theory for her house in San Jose, California, and its unusual architectural features such as "The Door to Nowhere" and repetitions of the number 13, is that she was a well-educated, inventive, and grieving widow in a time of limited societal options for women, and her great deal of time and money allowed her to explore her amateur interest in architecture (and thereby to support her workers and their families)—and that the house suffered damage in the 1906 earthquake. Sarah lived until 1922, at which point the house (one of her several properties) became the Winchester Mystery House tourist attraction it remains today.

Oliver Winchester, Sarah's father-in-law, made his wealth as a shirt manufacturer, and went on to invest in the Volcanic Repeating Arms Company, later the New Haven Arms Company, and then the Winchester Repeating Arms Company. B. Tyler Henry, who had formerly worked, among other things, as sewing machine mechanic, designed the company's breakthrough repeating rifle in 1860. Although the Henry Rifle was called "the most effective weapon ever made," Civil War sales were slow, and Oliver Winchester worked to promote the repeating rifles for use in Westward expansion. In 1873, the Winchester company premiered the centerfire Winchester Model 1873, which became known as "The Gun That Won the West." It and later models were touted by traveling sharpshooters such as the Topperweins.

"Claims" uses quotations from and references to the Spirit Sightings Log on the Winchester Mystery House website; its final section references Thomas Hardy's poem "The Voice"

"Repeater" "Buffalo Bill's Wild West," "Elizabeth 'Plinky' Topperwein," and "B. Tyler Henry" draw, among other sources, on *Winchester: The Gun That Won* the West, by Harold F. Williamson; "Repeater," "L.C. Smith and Bros." and "Winchester .351" also draw on Winchester company advertisements and correspondence (McCracken Research Library archives). For overall firearm and Winchester context, I am also indebted to *The Guns That Won the West: Firearms on the American Frontier, 1848-1898* by John Walter; *American Rifle: A Biography* by Alexander Rose; and *Winchester: An American Legend* by R.L. Wilson.

"Artizan Street, New Haven, 1850s: Sarah Winchester Reflects" and other poems draw on Mary Jo Ignoffo's invaluable biography *Captive of the Labyrinth*. Additional sources on Sarah and her house include *Lady of Mystery (Sarah Winchester)* by Ralph Rambo; *The Winchester Mystery House* guidebooks; "Sarah Winchester and Her House: How a Legend Grows" by Bruce Spoon; *The Inscrutable Mrs. Winchester and Her Mysterious Mansion* by Lisa L. Selby; internet posts; Jeremy Blake's video installation "Winchester Redux," which first got me interested in the house; and Winchester Mystery House tours

"Rehearsed by Sorrows" takes its title from the Galway Kinnell poem "Wait"

"How It Happened" references stories about Dr. Norman Baker's hospital at the Crescent Hotel in Eureka Springs, Arkansas

"Range," which is for Thoa and Lyndon, references Richard Wilbur's "Love Calls Us to the Things of This World," Italo Calvino's *The Baron in the Trees,* and T.S. Eliot's "The Hollow Men"

"Ammunition" draws on various sources, including historical materials on the Oare Gunpowder Works website

"Safe As Houses" was inspired by Caleb Brown's painting "Ayer House"; Herodotus, the Greek historian of the 5th century B.C., is often called The Father of History

"Transcontinental" is deeply indebted for context and quotations (including most of "Ferguson's Diary") to Stephen E. Ambrose's *Nothing Like It in the World,* as well as Library of Congress online articles; the Jack Morrow section relies on online sources about Arundel Hull

"The Barbed Wire Bible" quotes from the *The Living Gita* commentary by Sri Swami Satchidananda and the White Oaks School House museum in White Oaks, New Mexico

"Reconstruction" and "Spiritualists' Iniquities Unmasked" draw on *Spiritualism and Nineteenth-Century Letters* by Russell M. and Clare R. Goldfarb. *Spiritualits' Iniquities Unmasked* is the title of an 1859 pamphlet criticizing aspects of Spiritualism; the Fox sisters, who as children began to hear a spirit rapping on the walls of their family's New York farmhouse, helped begin the Spiritualist craze in the U.S. in the 1850s, and were alternately praised and criticized as frauds throughout their lives

"Sand Creek Testimony" draws on The Buffalo Bill Historical Center's Plains Indians Museum, and various accounts of the Sand Creek Massacre

"Many A Goat" follows the *Van Gogh: The Life* theory that Van Gogh's death may not have been suicide, but a shooting

"Widowed" is in memory of my maternal grandmother, Marian Berry

"Stereoscope: California" references photographs in *California in Depth: A Stereoscopic History* by Jim Crain

"Calamity Jane" was inspired by accounts of Calamity Jane's crossdressing, and by Oliver Winchester's history as a shirt manufacturer.

"Ghost Tours: Diamond Bessie"'s sources include "The Lonesome Death of Diamond Bessie" by John Troesser

"*Bison Bison*" draws on "Buffalo in Golden Gate Park" (Golden Gate Park website) and on images and quotations at the Buffalo Bill Historical Center

"Winchester .351 High-Power Self-Loading Rifle" quotes, in italics, a 1909 ad in *The American Field.*

Acknowledgements

Much gratitude to the editors of the following journals and anthologies for publishing this work (sometimes in earlier versions):

Barrow Street: "The Feet of Ghosts"; *Blackbird:* "Range" (as "Winchester") and "Clue"; *The Cimarron Review:* "Command Performance" and "Spiritualists' Iniquities Unmasked"; *Codex:* "Fortune"; *Conte:* "Many a Goat"; *The Cortland Review:* "Ghost Tours: Diamond Bessie"; *Poems Dead and Undead (Everyman's Library):* "Sarah Winchester, 23 Years Dead, Watches *House of Dracula*"; *FIELD:* "The Barbed Wire Bible" and "How It Happened" (II) (as "Survivor's Guilt"); *Gulf Coast:* "Whole Cloth"; *Hayden's Ferry Review:* "The Journalists Set the Record Straight on Sarah Winchester"; *Mid-American Review:* "Sarah Winchester, 23 Years Dead, Watches *House of Dracula*"; *The Missouri Review:* "Buffalo Bill's Wild West," "My Mother Reads to Her Daughters: *Great Expectations*," "Sarah Winchester Reads *Great Expectations*," "Sand Creek Testimony," "Repeater"; *Moon City Review:* "Rehearsed by Sorrows"; *New California Writing 2013:* "The House That Doesn't Grow" (I); *99 Poems for the 99 Percent:* "Port of Oakland"; *Poetic Research:* "Artizan Street," "Ammunition," and "Stereoscope: Annie Oakley and Sarah Winchester"; *Prairie Schooner:* "B. Tyler Henry"; *Quarterly West:* "Ghost Tours: Asphodel Plantation, 1975"; *The Seattle Review:* "The Blueprint," "The House That Doesn't Grow" (I and II), "The Door to Nowhere" (I and II), "Claims," "How It Happened" (I), and "The General Store Proprietor"; *Southern Poetry Review:* "Reconstruction" and "Port of Oakland"; *The Southern Review:* "Ghost Tours: Houdini"; *Subtropics*: "Widowed," "*Bison Bison*," and "American Progress"; *32 Poems:* "Winchester .351 Self-Loading Rifle"; *Threepenny Review:* "John Brown, First Proprietor of the Winchester Mystery House, Explains"; *Western Humanities Review,* "Safe as Houses," "Stereoscope: California," and "Calamity Jane, Somewhat Inebriated, Thinks of Writing to Oliver Winchester"; *Willow Springs:* "Transcontinental"; *ZYZZYVA*, "Sarah Winchester, 46 Years Dead, Talks to Andy Warhol" and "L.C. Smith, Makers of Fine Guns and Typewriters, Advertise"

Deep thanks to the National Endowment for the Arts for a 2011 fellowship that gave me crucial encouragement and time to write and research; to University of Idaho for a 2012 Seed Grant; to The Buffalo Bill Historical Center and McCracken Research Library, particularly Mary Robinson and her staff, as well as Jim Reed and the staff at the History San Jose Archives for facilitating pivotal research. To Maria Hummel, Keith Ekiss, Sara Michas-Martin, Rita Mae Reese, David Thacker, Daniel Berkner, Warren Bromley-Vogel, Jill McDonough, Elizabeth Bradfield, John Nieves, Stacy Isenbarger, and Abigail Ulman for invaluable feedback and creative conversations. To the Stegner Fellows, Eavan Boland, W.S. DiPiero, Ken Fields, William Logan, and Sidney Wade for enduring teachings. To Sam Ligon for his editing of "Transcontinental"; to Robert Wrigley, Joy Passanante, Gary Williams, and my other colleagues, students, and friends at UI and University of Arkansas; as well as my father, Raymond, my stepmother, Bonnie, and my other family, for believing in me and this project. Deep thanks also to the many authors and historians whose work I relied on; to the Winchester House; to my editor, Gabe Fried, and everyone at Persea. To my mother. To Sarah Winchester. And finally Dylan Champagne—who has lived with my ghosts, and helped me build more wisely, every step of the way.